Snap books®

Drawing Fun

HOW TO DRAW Cool Fashions

by Kathryn Clay

illustrated by Julia Nielsen

Capstone press®

Mankato, Minnesota

Snap Books are published by Capstone Press,
151 Good Counsel Drive, P.O. Box 669, Mankato, Minnesota 56002.
www.capstonepress.com

Books published by Capstone Press are manufactured with paper
containing at least 10 percent post-consumer waste.

Library of Congress Cataloging-in-Publication Data
Clay, Kathryn.
    How to draw cool fashions / by Kathryn Clay; illustrated by Julia Nielsen.
    p. cm. — (Snap books. Drawing fun)
    Summary: "Lively text and fun illustrations describe how to draw cool fashions" — Provided by publisher.
    Includes bibliographical references and index.
    ISBN 978-1-4296-3406-9 (library binding)
    1. Fashion drawing — Juvenile literature. I. Nielsen, Julia. II. Title. III. Series.
TT509.C524 2010
741.6'72 — dc22   2009005991

Credits
Juliette Peters, designer

Photo Credits
Capstone Press/TJ Thoraldson Digital Photography, 4 (pencil), 5 (all), 32 (pencil)

Table of Contents

Getting Started 4

Must-Have Materials.............. 5

Trendy 6

Formal 8

Athletic 10

1970s Retro 12

Skater 14

Asian 16

1920s Retro 18

Winter 20

Summer................................. 22

All about Accessories........ 24

Punk 26

Glossary 30

Read More 31

Internet Sites 31

Index..................................... 32

Getting Started

Are you more likely to pick up a fashion magazine than your math book? Do you watch awards shows just to check out what everyone's wearing? Is your closet full of the latest trends? If you're fascinated by fashion, sharpen your pencils, and get ready to draw your own stylish designs.

What fashions catch your eye? If you're into the latest sassy styles, check out the trendy outfit. Do you love the retro look? Try drawing a vintage dress from the 1970s. Maybe you can't resist gorgeous gowns? Then the formal style is for you. With your unique style and the instructions in this book, you'll be drawing these awesome outfits in no time.

Of course, fashion trends don't stay the same for long. But once you've mastered some of the styles in this book, you'll be able to draw all kinds of cool couture. Let your inner fashionista take over, and see what kinds of fun fashions you can create.

Must-Have Materials

1. First you'll need something to draw on. Any blank, white paper will work well.

2. Pencils are a must for these drawing projects. Be sure to keep a bunch nearby.

3. Because sharp pencils make clean lines, you'll be sharpening those pencils a lot. Have a pencil sharpener handy.

4. Even the best artist needs to erase a line now and then. Pencil erasers wear out fast. A rubber or kneaded eraser will last much longer.

5. To make your drawings pop off the page, use colored pencils or markers.

Trendy

This totally trendy look works for everything from a shopping trip on Rodeo Drive to a star-studded movie premiere. It combines a crisp pair of skinny jeans and a cute cami. Complete the look with a half-jacket in an eye-catching color.

Dress up this style by switching out the jeans with a denim miniskirt.

STEP 1

STEP 2

STEP 3

STEP 4

Formal

Hit a glam slam with a shimmering formal. This floor-sweeping gown is a classic A-line shape that flares out at the waist. A dress like this is sure to turn heads at weddings, proms, or red-carpet events.

Formal doesn't always mean full-length. Try drawing a short A-line dress with a halter top.

STEP 1

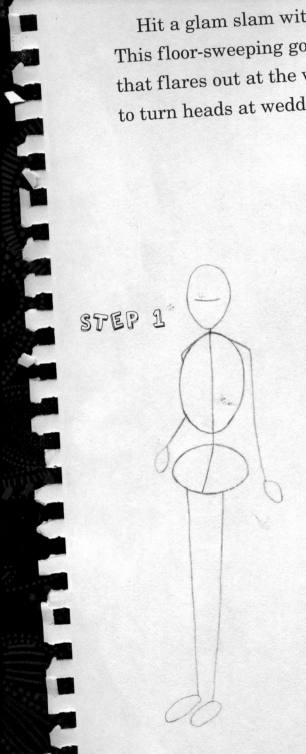

STEP 2

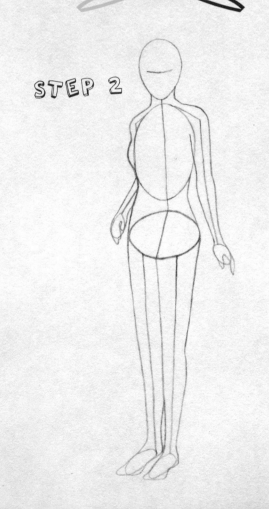

STEP 3

STEP 4

Athletic

You don't have to sacrifice style when you're working up a sweat. Comfortable workout clothes can also make a fashion statement. Draw this active athlete sporting a matching tank top and yoga pants.

Now get this girl ready for a run. Add a nylon jacket, pants, and stylish sneakers.

STEP 1

STEP 2

STEP 3

STEP 4

1970s Retro

Designers love to recreate old looks and turn them into modern trends. This look borrows from the 1970s. The fringed suede boots, low-slung belt, and skinny headband are definite blasts from the past.

Try drawing other retro fashions like bell-bottom pants and platform shoes.

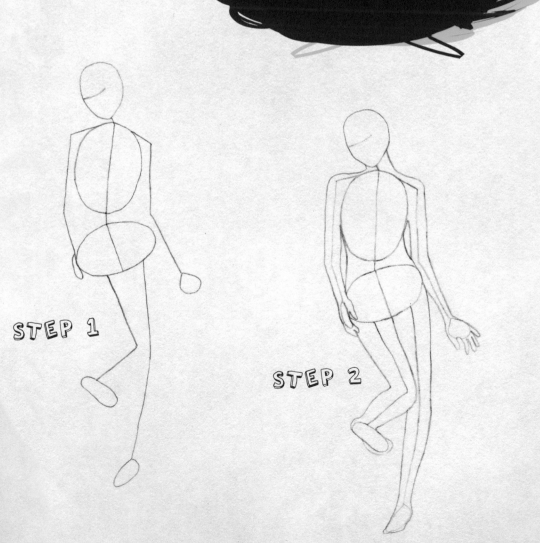

STEP 1

STEP 2

STEP 3

STEP 4

Skater

Skaters set their own trends with clothing that's more about comfort than fashion. Loose-fitting styles don't get in the way when skaters are showing off their cool moves. Add some color with a bold animal print and flat-soled skater shoes.

Now draw a skater boy. Give him a baggy hoodie, loose-fitting jeans, and a knit cap.

STEP 1

STEP 2

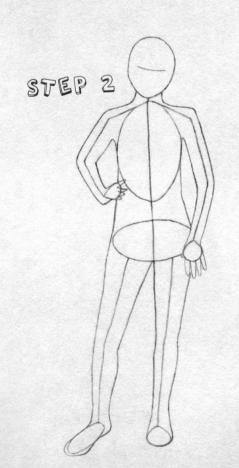

STEP 4

Asian

Going global is always in style. This Asian-inspired design takes its cue from a traditional Japanese kimono. Its bright red color and detailed butterfly print make this sleeveless dress hard to miss. A matching wrap completes the look.

To modify this dress, simply change the design. Other traditional Asian designs include birds and flowers.

STEP 1

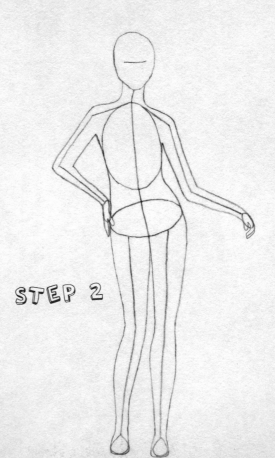

STEP 2

STEP 3

STEP 4

1920s Retro

After almost 100 years, the 1920s flapper dress is still turning heads. This tiered minidress is a modern version of a vintage fashion. The bright colors and knee-high boots give this style a contemporary twist.

Top off this look with a cloche (KLAWSH) hat. This fitted, bell-shaped hat from the 1920s is back in style.

STEP 1

STEP 2

STEP 3

STEP 4

Winter

Fashion designers are all about looking cool while staying warm. The secret is lots of stylish layers. This girl is showing off a black peacoat over purple leggings. Her matching hat and gloves are practical and chic. The look is completed with a trendy pair of boots.

Try drawing a comfy sweaterdress and black leggings.

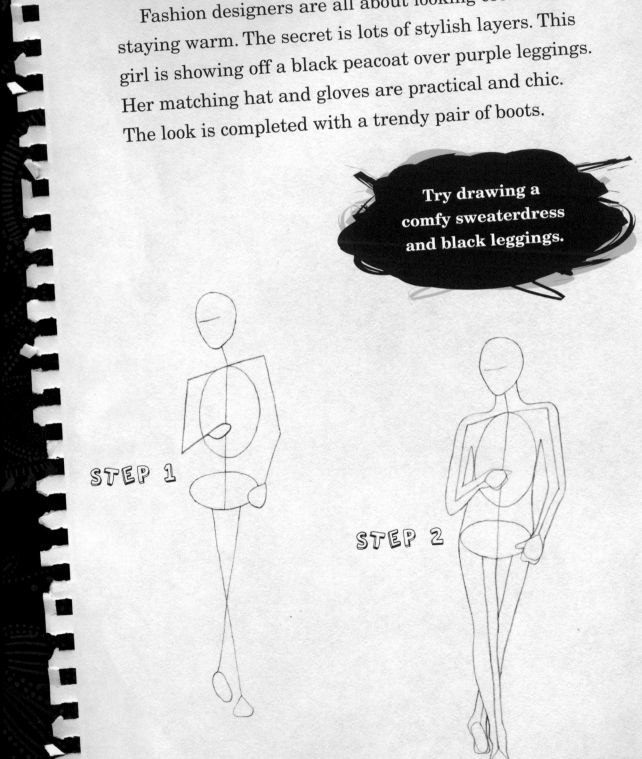

STEP 1

STEP 2

STEP 3

STEP 4

Summer

Summer is the perfect time to show off a short, sassy style. This strappy sundress is just the trick. To personalize the look, add some colorful bracelets and a pair of kitten heels.

Take this outfit from day to night. Just add a button-down cardigan and a patterned scarf.

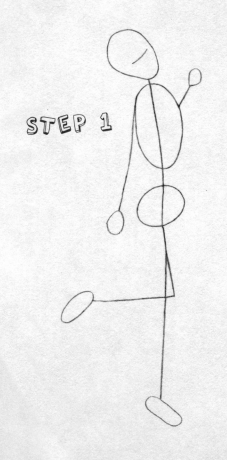

STEP 1

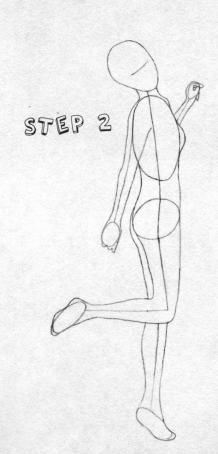

STEP 2

STEP 3

STEP 4

All about Accesories

Sometimes a stylish outfit is more about the accessories than the clothes. This look starts out with a basic pair of low-rise jeans and a long-sleeved tee. Edgy accessories like a colorful scarf and belt make this style sizzle. Add a matching purse and baseball cap as final, flashy touches.

Try switching up the accessories. Replace the scarf and purse with hoop earrings and a chunky necklace.

STEP 1

STEP 2

STEP 3

STEP 4

Punk

Coordinating punk outfits make this couple a fashionable pair. The guy is sporting corduroy pants, a plain black tee, and a jean jacket. She's showing off a plaid skirt, athletic socks, and a combo tank top T-shirt. Both complete their look with matching celeb shades.

This couple loves to stay ahead of fashion trends. Give them a new look by creating a style that's all your own.

STEP 1

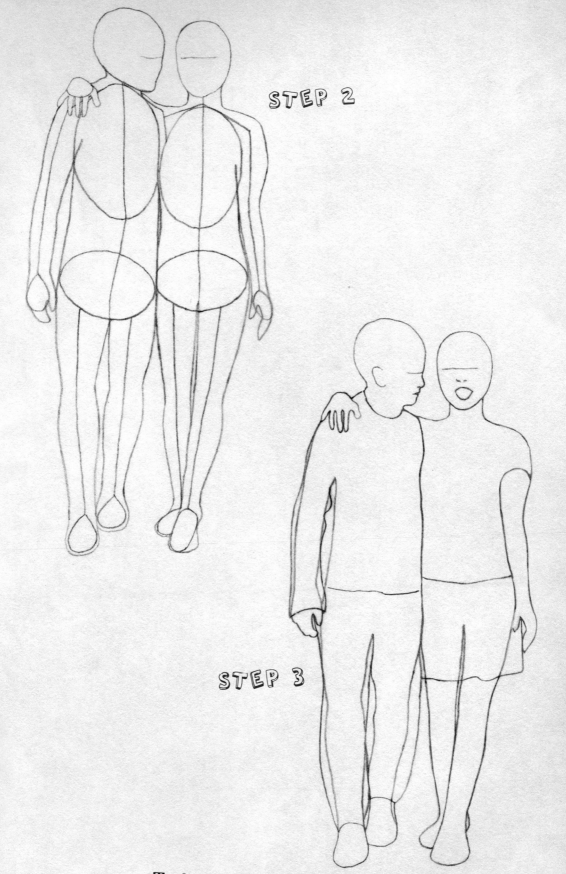

STEP 2

STEP 3

To finish this drawing, turn to the next page. ➡

STEP 4

STEP 5

Glossary

chic (SHEEK) — a fashionable style

couture (koo-TUR) — fashionable clothing that is custom-made

fashionista (FASH-uhn-ees-ta) — someone who works in or has strong knowledge of fashion

flapper (FLAP-er) — a young woman, during the 1920s, who behaved and dressed in a bold and original manner

kimono (kee-MOH-no) — a long, loose robe with wide sleeves and a sash

premiere (pruh-MIHR) — the first public performance of a film, play, or work of music or dance

trend (TREND) — new fashion or the direction in which things are changing

unique (yoo-NEEK) — one of a kind

vintage (VIN-tij) — from the past

Read More

Clay, Kathryn. *How to Draw Cool Kids*. Drawing Fun. Mankato, Minn.: Capstone Press, 2009.

Hart, Christopher. *How to Draw Chic Fashions*. How to Draw. New York: Watson Guptill, 2006.

Jones, Jen. *Fashion Design School: Learning the Skills to Succeed*. World of Fashion. Mankato, Minn.: Capstone Press, 2007.

Internet Sites

FactHound offers a safe, fun way to find Internet sites related to this book. All of the sites on FactHound have been researched by our staff.

Here's all you do:

Visit *www.facthound.com*

FactHound will fetch the best sites for you!

Index

1920s retro, 18
1970s retro, 4, 12

all about accessories, 24
Asian, 16
athletic, 10

cloche hat, 18

drawing supplies, 5

formal, 4, 8

layers, 20

punk, 26

skater, 14
summer, 22

trendy, 4, 6

vintage, 4, 18

winter, 20